At the Market

by Callie McCafferty

PEARSON

Glenview, Illinois • Boston, Massachusetts
Chandler, Arizona • Upper Saddle River, New Jersey

This is a market.
It is big!

It is time to shop.
What can we get?

We can get peppers.

We like lemons.
We can get some.

What can we get?

We can get fruit.

It is time to pay.
Then it is time to eat.